Color!

Whimsical Fancies
Adult Coloring Book

Deb Gilbert

Heller
Brothers
Publishing

Title: Color! Whimsical Fancies Adult Coloring Book
Author: Deb Gilbert
Published by: Heller Brothers Publishing
Cover Design © 2016 by graphichubs
Copyright © 2016 by Deb Gilbert
Photo Credits: OlgaDrozd@depositphotos.com

First Edition, 2016
Published in USA

ISBN 978-1944678-04-3

ISBN 978-1-944678-04-3

5 1 2 9 9 >

9 781944 678043

This Coloring Book Belongs To:

_____

Date Completed: _____

Media Used:_____

_____

_____

Notes: _____

_____

_____

_____

_____

_____

Date Completed: _____

Media Used:_____

_____

_____

Notes: _____

_____

_____

_____

_____

_____

Date Completed: _____

Media Used:_____

_____

_____

Notes: _____

_____

_____

_____

_____

Date Completed: _____

Media Used:_____

_____

_____

Notes: _____

_____

_____

_____

_____

Date Completed: _____
Media Used:_____
_____
_____
Notes: _____
_____
_____
_____
_____
_____

Date Completed: _____

Media Used:_____

_____

_____

Notes: _____

_____

_____

_____

_____

_____

Date Completed: _____

Media Used:_____

_____

_____

Notes: _____

_____

_____

_____

_____

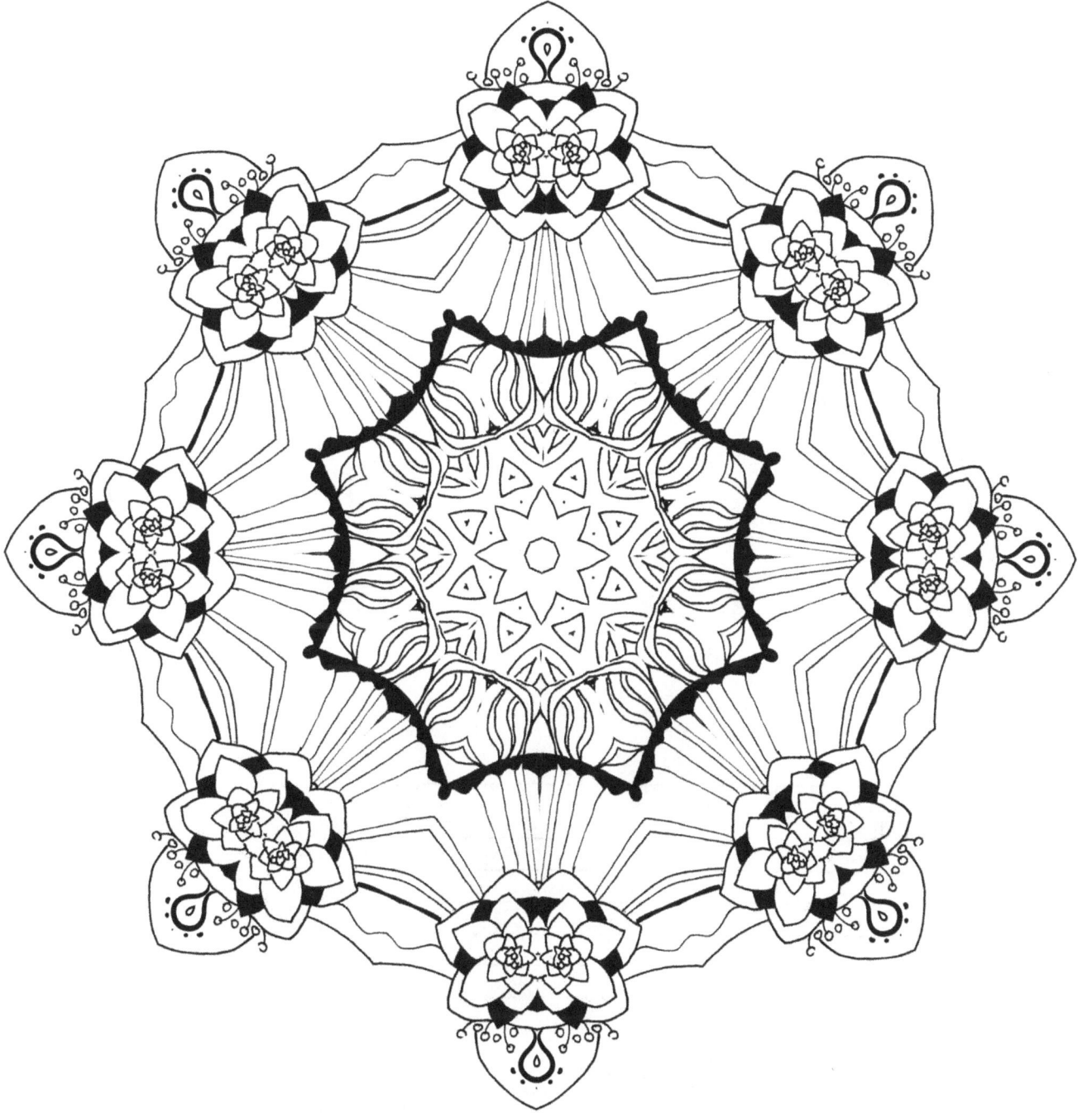

Date Completed: _____

Media Used:_____

_____

_____

Notes: _____

_____

_____

_____

_____

Date Completed: _____
Media Used:_____
_____
_____
Notes: _____
_____
_____
_____
_____

Date Completed: _____
Media Used:_____
_____
_____
Notes: _____
_____
_____
_____
_____

Date Completed: _____

Media Used:_____

_____

_____

Notes: _____

_____

_____

_____

_____

Date Completed: _____

Media Used:_____

_____

_____

Notes: _____

_____

_____

_____

_____

Date Completed: _____

Media Used:_____

_____

_____

Notes: _____

_____

_____

_____

_____

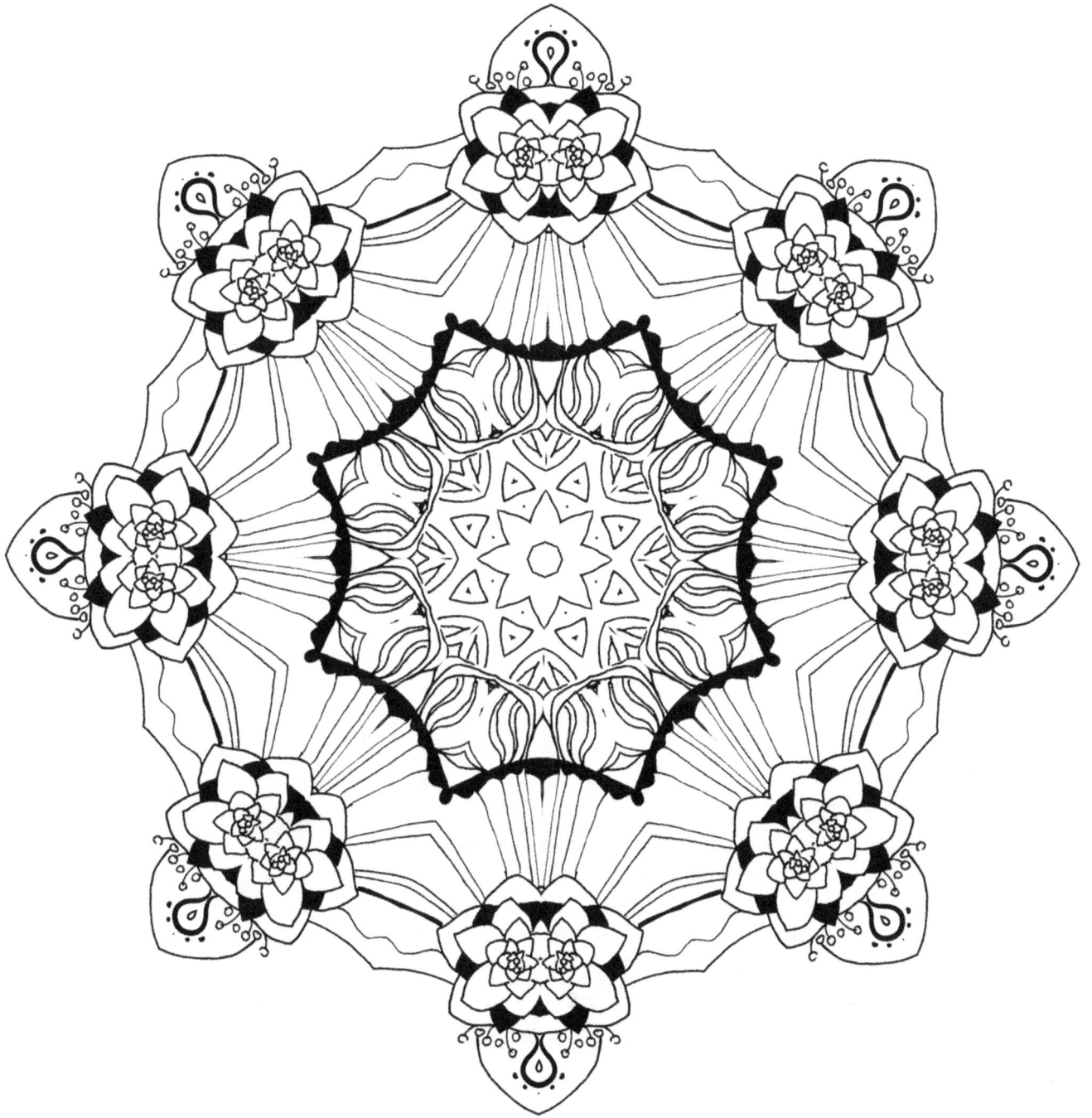

Date Completed: _____
Media Used:_____
_____
_____
Notes: _____
_____
_____
_____
_____
_____

Date Completed: _____

Media Used:_____

_____

_____

Notes: _____

_____

_____

_____

_____

Date Completed: _____

Media Used:_____

_____

_____

Notes: _____

_____

_____

_____

_____

Date Completed: _____

Media Used:_____

_____

_____

Notes: _____

_____

_____

_____

_____

_____

Date Completed: _____

Media Used:_____

_____

_____

Notes: _____

_____

_____

_____

_____

Date Completed: _____

Media Used:_____

_____

_____

Notes: _____

_____

_____

_____

_____

Date Completed: _____

Media Used:_____

_____

_____

Notes: _____

_____

_____

_____

_____

Date Completed: _____

Media Used:_____

_____

_____

Notes: _____

_____

_____

_____

_____

_____

Date Completed: _____

Media Used:_____

_____

_____

Notes: _____

_____

_____

_____

_____

Date Completed: _____
Media Used:_____
_____
_____
Notes: _____
_____
_____
_____
_____

Date Completed: _____

Media Used:_____

_____

_____

Notes: _____

_____

_____

_____

_____

Date Completed: _____

Media Used:_____

_____

_____

Notes: _____

_____

_____

_____

_____

Date Completed: _____

Media Used: _____

_____

_____

Notes: _____

_____

_____

_____

_____

Date Completed: _____

Media Used:_____

_____

_____

Notes: _____

_____

_____

_____

_____

Date Completed: _____

Media Used:_____

_____

_____

Notes: _____

_____

_____

_____

_____

Date Completed: _____

Media Used:_____

_____

_____

Notes: _____

_____

_____

_____

_____

Date Completed: _____
Media Used:_____
_____
_____
Notes: _____
_____
_____
_____
_____
_____

Date Completed: _____
Media Used:_____
_____
_____
Notes: _____
_____
_____
_____
_____

Date Completed: _____

Media Used:_____

_____

_____

Notes: _____

_____

_____

_____

_____

Date Completed: _____

Media Used:_____

_____

_____

Notes: _____

_____

_____

_____

_____

Date Completed: _____
Media Used:_____
_____
_____
Notes: _____
_____
_____
_____
_____

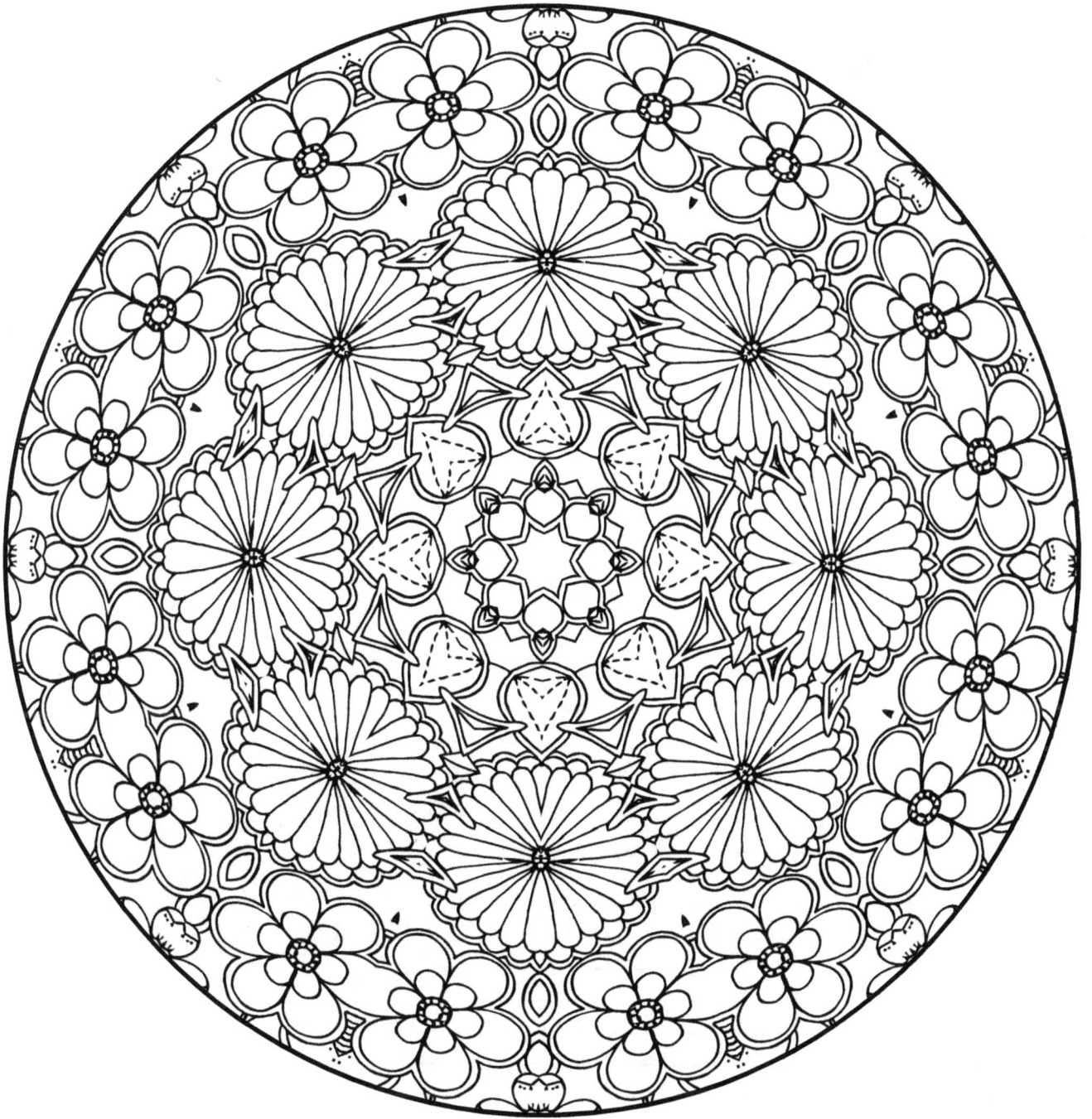

Date Completed: _____

Media Used:_____

_____

_____

Notes: _____

_____

_____

_____

_____

About the Author

Dr. Deb Gilbert has been working from home since 2007 and is an online professor of education, research, and leadership. She has been involved in public schools and higher education for over 25 years and has a passion for promoting literacy.

For more information on Deb Gilbert, please join her at
www.hellerbrotherspublishing.com
and on Facebook at:
https://www.facebook.com/coloringbookstoheal

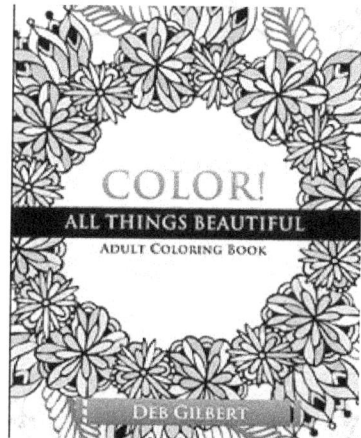